Images of Ourselves

The Faith and Work of Canadian Women

Images of Ourselves

The Faith and Work of Canadian Women

Compiled by
The Canadian Ecumenical Decade Co-ordinating Group for
The Ecumenical Decade of Churches in Solidarity with Women
in Church and Society

Photographs by Pamela Harris

ECUMENICAL DECADE
CHURCHES IN SOLIDARITY
WITH WOMEN
1988-1998

Grateful acknowledgement is made for permission to reprint from the following copyrighted material:

From *Meditations with Hildegard of Bingen* by Gabrielle Uhlein, ©1983, and from *Meditations with Mechtild of Magdeburg* by Sue Woodruff, ©1982, both used by permission of Bear & Co., Santa Fe, NM.

From *L'autre Parole*, "Magnificat" by L'autre Parole Collectif (March 1986); "En Mémoire D'elles" by Denyse Joubert-Nantel (March 1990); "Ballade des Exilées" by Marie Gratton Boucher (September 1989), reprinted with permission.

I Am No Longer Afraid and *Roots and Wings*, ©Linnea Good, reprinted with permission.

The photographs on pages 6, 22, 30, 34, 42, 57, 63, 80, 86, 92, 94, 112, 117, and 122 are from Pamela Harris's *Faces of Feminism*, to be published by Second Story Press.

The United Church Publishing House, 85 St. Clair Avenue East, Toronto, Ontario M4T 1M8

Publisher: R.L. Naylor
Editor-in-Chief: Peter Gordon White
Editorial Assistant: Elizabeth Phinney
Book Design: Saskia Rowley, Graphics and Print Production
Printed in Canada by: Gagné Printing

Cover photo: Patricia MacKay and Judith Arbus at a women's celebration, Toronto.

Canadian Cataloguing in Publication Data

Main entry under title:
Images of ourselves
Includes some text in French.
ISBN 0-919000-99-1

1. Women - Prayer-books and devotions - English.
2. Meditations. 3. Women in Christianity - Canada.
I. Canadian Ecumenical Decade Co-ordinating Group.

BV4844.I53 1992   242'.843   C92-093386-6

Contents

Preface

A word about how this book came into being.

In 1988, when the World Council of Churches proclaimed the Ecumenical Decade of Churches in Solidarity with Women in Church and Society, some women in Canada came together to consider how they could support, encourage, and assist involvement across Canada and throughout the denominations in what the World Council declared as the aims of the Decade:

• Empowering women to challenge oppressive structures in the global community, their country, and their church;

• Affirming — through shared leadership and decision-making, theology, and spirituality — the decisive contributions of women in churches and communities;

• Giving visibility to women's perspectives and actions in the work and struggle for justice, peace, and the integrity of creation;

• Enabling the churches to free themselves from racism, sexism, and classism; from teachings and practices that discriminate against women;

• Encouraging the churches to take actions in solidarity with women.

The Co-ordinating Group has functioned since with official appointees from denominations and volunteers.

In January 1990, this group appointed a committee to produce a book of worship resources, meditations, and devotional material written by women across Canada. It wanted a book that would be ecumenical in nature, that would provide an opportunity for women to express their faith, and that would reflect through a variety of topics the experience of women's lives across Canada.

The contributions chosen by the committee come from women in nine provinces and in seven denominations: Anglican, Baptist, Disciples of Christ, Lutheran, Presbyterian, Roman Catholic, and United Church.

Our membership has fluctuated for various reasons, but each person involved made valuable contributions to the development of the book. Our sincere thanks goes to Caroline Wilkinson and Janette Ledwith who helped us get started; Edith Shore who saw us through most of the work and provided valuable advice; Barbara Hillis who recorded many of our meetings; and Marta Condolo, who worked on the committee from beginning to end.

A very special thank you to our editors, June Stevenson and Rebekah Chevalier, for their careful work and caring support and encouragement.

Our appreciation is expressed also to June Stevenson and Katherine Allen for typing the manuscript.

We deeply appreciate the willingness of Dr. Nancy Cocks and Dr. Ray Hodgson to provide theological comment on some of the manuscripts, when requested.

Janet MacPherson, the national programme co-ordinator of the Co-ordinating Group, deserves a special vote of thanks for handling the initial correspondence soliciting submissions. We also appreciate the time of Nancy Whitla, who read through and commented on the completed manuscript.

Those who made submissions, even though all could not be included, deserve special thanks and appreciation for participating so readily in this project. Without them there would be no book.

Barbara Woodruff
Convener of the Editorial Committee
The Canadian Ecumenical Decade Co-ordinating Group

Why We Need Another Decade for Women

Anne M. Squire

At Easter time in 1988, the World Council of Churches launched the Ecumenical Decade of Churches in Solidarity with Women in Church and Society. Although the United Nations Decade for Women had recently ended, many inequities still faced women in society and particularly in the church. For example:

• In times of economic recession, women are the first to be thrown out of work.

• Women workers are not only among the lowest paid, but are often exploited by being hired part time with no benefits or protection.

• Famine is hardest on women, who bear the heaviest responsibility for the family.

• Rural women receive the least attention in development plans and are not consulted about their needs.

• As socio-economic conditions deteriorate, the frustration of jobless men leads to increased sexual abuse and violence against women.

• Growing poverty and the promotion of sex-tourism have greatly increased the plague of prostitution, especially among younger women.

• Among the victims of nuclear testing, especially in the South Pacific, are the women who bear the burden of increased miscarriages and deformed children.

The World Council thought it was time that churches became involved in addressing these issues, as well as the inequities in church structures that make it difficult for many women to share in the total life of the church. For example, some denominations still do not permit women to be ordained, and in many denominations, women (who make up the majority of church members) are inadequately represented on governing boards.

When we begin to probe the reasons women have been undervalued in the churches, we realize with dismay that one reason has been the teaching of the church itself. That teaching has been based on an understanding and interpretation of scripture that has until recent years gone unchallenged.

Those who developed our early theology pointed to scripture that functioned to keep women in their place. The early theologians made Eve the scapegoat for both Adam's fall and the entry of sin into the world. They claimed that the body of a man is as superior to that of a woman as the soul is to the body. Indeed, women were seen as misbegotten males with mental and moral as well as physical inferiority.

The two very different stories of creation in the first two chapters of Genesis provide an example of how scripture, the interpretation of scripture, and the authority given to scripture have been used to keep women subservient. In Genesis 1 there is an attempt to hold up a vision of the created universe as God saw it, "and God saw that it was good." In Genesis 2 there is an attempt to explain why the world was not as God saw it, why sin had entered paradise, why women were subservient to men, why men had to toil for a living, and women had to suffer in childbirth.

Two stories — two versions of creation — so different in their description of how males and females were created, and so different in their influence on relationships between women and men. The church chose to emphasize the second story in which Eve blames the snake for tempting her and Adam blames both the woman and God for his temptation. It is in this second story that woman is designated as a helpmeet for man, a term which has been used to justify her subservience, although the original Hebrew word actually means "help like that given by God" and thus implies superiority rather than inferiority.

Women have had to live with that legacy until recent times, when they began to develop theologies that gave a place to women's experience and to untangle the web that has held them subservient. As we study scripture, we find the roots of a struggle that, for men, became a struggle for power, and for women, a struggle for recognition as persons who had every right to be counted as people of God. For even though women were left uncounted in the census (Num. 1-4; 26-27) and ignored in the counting of those who were fed by Jesus (Matt. 14:20), there is evidence in scripture that in God's eyes women were important. Parts of scripture speak of women's heroic deeds, use feminine imagery for God, tell of women's ministry in the early church. These parts have been overlooked. Instead, the parts that have been emphasized tell a woman to keep silent in church and to accept a lesser role than her husband.

Part of our responsibility as Christians is to denounce any system, religious or otherwise, that functions to justify and sanctify an unjust social order. We keep before us a vision of the time when God's reign of justice and peace will hold sway. That vision was part of the baptismal formula of the early church, though it somehow became lost in the power struggles through the centuries. Paul, in his letter to the Galatians, reminds us that being Christian means working for a time when there shall be no distinction between slave and free, man and woman, Jew and Greek, because we all will be one in Christ (Gal. 3:28).

When we hear an appeal to scripture to justify patriarchy, we must remember our history. Similar appeals have been used to justify persecution of the Jews, the burning of those labelled witches, the torture of so-called heretics, national wars in Europe, the subhuman conditions of African slavery, and the horrors of apartheid. Any appeal to scripture must rest firmly on that central core which points to the rule of a just and compassionate God.

A key point for women has been the question of power and how it is exercised in church and society. Because a woman's physical power is usually less than that of a man, women have been subject to rape, incest, and physical abuse. Because a woman's economic power is generally less than that of a man, poverty bears a female face. The poorest of the poor are single mothers and elderly women. And yet it is men who, for the most part, are the lawmakers, who make decisions affecting our lives, who exercise power over women.

The kind of power women seek is not power *over* but power *to* — the kind of power that seeks to empower others, the kind of power that is shared, the kind of power that is the opposite of the hierarchical models that still dictate so much of women's existence.

That is really what the Ecumenical Decade is all about. Its aim is to encourage local groups, churches, and denominations to look at the situation of women honestly and to do what we can locally and globally to change it. This may mean looking at the scriptures to see where patriarchy obscures the gospel message, acknowledging this, and sharing the good news with others. It may mean rejecting any theology that makes women less than persons and accepting instead a theology that affirms the contributions of women. It may mean looking at our own churches to see where sexism still exists and doing our part in eradicating it. It may mean celebrating what has already been accomplished and giving visibility to women's perspectives and to the actions of women who work for peace, justice, and the integrity of creation. It may mean pledging ourselves to support women around the world whose situations are often so much worse than our own. It will mean working with men to make changes, because the church cannot be in solidarity with women until men and women take action together.

The Ecumenical Decade is not a programme; it is a process, an opportunity for churches to build on what has already happened and to work for that day when women and men are the whole people of God.

Anne Squire is a former moderator of The United Church of Canada.

The Cronies,
Women's Support
Group, Winnipeg.

Who Will Roll Away the Stone?

Lois Klempa

The theme the World Council of Churches chose to introduce the Ecumenical Decade is the question the women who were first to visit Jesus' tomb asked one another on that first Easter morning: Who will roll away the stone for us? (Mark 16:3).

It was an obvious question. But they went anyway. They went knowing there was a large stone blocking the entrance to the tomb, which they would have no way of moving. They might have said to each other, "What is the use of going? We will never be able to move that stone. Maybe we should wait for the men." No. They went anyway — and found the stone had already been rolled away.

From these women who went to the tomb on that first Easter morning, we learn the importance of venturing out in faith, of setting forth not knowing where God will lead us, but trusting that God goes before us, removing stones and obstacles that seem to us insurmountable.

As women in the church, we face many obstacles, many stones. And it is very easy to become discouraged, to ask, what is the use? The situation is impossible. We might as well give up.

We thank God for those first women, disciples of Jesus, who would not give up. And we thank God for women who came later and continued to challenge even in the face of a church that was becoming increasingly more determined to keep women subordinate and silent. We realize what courage they must have had to carry on in spite of seemingly hopeless situations.

Throughout the history of the church, there have always been women who were willing to face persecution and ridicule because they believed God calls women to take their places beside men in the life and work of the church. They would not give up in spite of many obstacles, and they discovered, as women have through the ages, that Christ goes before, opening the way and beckoning onward.

Who will roll away the stone? An impossible task. But they went on anyway, and found that the stone had already been rolled away. So they entered the tomb, where they saw a young man sitting at the right wearing a white robe, and they were alarmed. "Don't be alarmed," he said.

Fear. There are many kinds of fear — fear of the unknown, fear of change, fear of venturing out in faith not knowing where we are going.

You must not be afraid. This is, I believe, a particularly appropriate message for women. Women are sometimes timid, lacking in confidence, afraid to speak out, unsure of themselves. Do not be afraid. This is a message we need to hear. We know how debilitating fear is, how it paralyzes us and makes us unable to act.

This is exactly what happened to the women in the story. Mark tells us they went out and ran from the tomb, distressed and terrified. They said nothing to anyone because they were afraid. Fortunately, they later seemed to overcome their fear. All four gospel writers tell us the women went and told the disciples that Jesus was alive: "You must not be afraid."

We do not know what the future holds. We venture into the unknown, but we know that the risen Christ is there before us, urging us into new and untried ways.

Do not be alarmed. I know you are looking for Jesus of Nazareth, who was crucified. He is not here. He has been raised. Now go ...

"Who will roll away the stone?" they asked one another. And they looked up and saw that the stone had already been rolled away.

O loving, caring Saviour. Sometimes we feel so frightened. Often we feel so inadequate, so uncertain. Should I? Shouldn't I? Is this the right thing to do? What will people think? Will they think I am stupid? Or weak? Will they laugh? We remember Mary Magdalene and the other women who carried the joyous message of your resurrection to the other disciples, and we thank you that they were able to overcome their fear. Make us strong. Make us daring. Above all, give us the faith to believe that Jesus Christ is the answer to this world's misery, and the courage to follow where he leads us. Amen.

Lois Klempa of Westmount, Que., is a graduate of Ewart College, Toronto, and has served on several boards and committees of the Presbyterian Church in Canada.

Grania Jones,
Toronto.

A Liturgy

Vivian Mancini

Song to the Spirit

Holy Spirit, making life alive, moving in all things,
root of all created being, cleansing the cosmos of every infirmity
effacing guilt, anointing wounds.
You are lustrous and praiseworthy light.
You waken and reawaken every thing that is. Amen.

Hildegard of Bingen

Reading

Who is the Holy Spirit?
The Holy Spirit is a compassionate outpouring
of the Creator
    and the Son.
This is why
    when we on earth
        pour out compassion and mercy
        from the depths of our hearts
    and give to the poor
    and dedicate our bodies to the service of the broken,
to that very extent
do we resemble the Holy Spirit.

Mechtild of Magdeburg

Prayer

Most beautiful, compassionate Spirit, you who brood over our universe with loving longing, teach us to be a compassionate people. Teach us your way of loving longing for justice, for truth, for unity, for a Spirit of unconditional love. We ask this through God, our tender mother, and through Jesus, our compassionate brother. Amen.

Reflecting

Spend a few minutes reflecting on one incident in your life when God's Spirit was especially apparent. Make this experience as vivid as possible by recalling how you felt and what emotions arose in you. What were the results of that special encounter? Allow yourself to praise and thank God for the gift of God's Spirit, who dwells with you.

Reading

As the Godhead
　　strikes the note
　　Humanity sings.
The Holy Spirit is the harpist
　　and all the strings must sound
　　　　which are strung in love.

Mechtild of Magdeburg

Response

Spirit of God, play on our souls as on a harp.
Teach us to respond in loving harmony
that flows to the entire universe.

Reading

The Holy Spirit flows
    through us
    with the marvelous
    Creative Power
of everlasting joy.

Mechtild of Magdeburg

Response

Spirit of joy, teach us the creative power of celebration;
of joy that is shared in love.

Reading

I once heard the Spirit speak to the Creator, saying:
    "We will no longer be unfruitful.
    We will have a creative kingdom."
And then I heard Jesus speak to the Creator, saying:
    "My nature too must bear fruit.
    Together we shall work wonders.
    So let us fashion human beings
    After the Pattern of myself."

Mechtild of Magdeburg

Response

Creative Spirit, you call us to the celebration of ourselves as co-creators. You invite us back to our creativity. You initiate our birthing into creating with you and each other a world of harmony and delight.

Give us of your wisdom and love, that creation through our lives will
bear delectable, delicious fruit.
Teach us the power of ecstasy.
We ask this through our living mother God, and our brother Jesus.
Amen.

Song to the Spirit

> Holy Spirit, making life alive, moving in all things,
> root of all created being, cleansing the cosmos of every infirmity,
> effacing guilt, anointing wounds.
> You are lustrous and praiseworthy light.
> You waken and reawaken every thing that is. Amen.

Hildegard of Bingen

Suggestions for using this liturgy in group worship

The group assembles in silence, while soft music is played. Pachelbel's
Canon is an appropriate example. The group is in a closed circle, with
a table in the centre on which there is a lighted candle and a green plant,
or a single rose. Slips of paper on the table contain a word describing
the gifts of the Spirit — i.e., wisdom, compassion, love, peace, justice.

Song to the Spirit may be read as a poem or sung as a hymn to the
music below, by Vivian Mancini.

After the time for reflection on personal experience, sharing the
experience is appropriate, should you wish to do so. When the sharing
is completed, each person takes a slip of paper from the table. The word
on the paper is the gift of the Spirit to be received, reflected upon, and
shared with others.

The prayer time which follows closes as the circle opens, a symbol of bringing our creative gifts to the universe. While the circle opens, the group sings again *Song to the Spirit*.

SONG TO THE SPIRIT

Words by Hildegard of Bingen
Music by Vivian Mancini S.C.

Ho - ly Spi - rit mak- ing life a - live_____ mov - ing in all things_____

_____ root of all cre - a - ted be - ing cleans - ing the cos -

- mos of eve - ry in - firm - i - ty e - ffa - cing guilt

a - noin - ting wounds. You are lust - rous and praise - worth - y light.

You wa-ken and re - a - wa-ken eve-ry thing that is A - - - men. _____

Vivian Mancini is director of Carmel Centre, a renewal centre in New Waterford, N.S.

*Ma Snooks
with her bread,
Trout River, Nfld.*

Eucharistic Prayer

Donna Kilarski

Out of silence
Your presence, God, already there
In pulsating ripples of timelessness.
Yet you stir from within
Surrounding all life
With your love.
    And you stir from within
    Surrounding all life
    With your love.

A seed planted deep in soil rich and black,
Trembling release of life:
Jesus among us;
Your love in earth;
In the darkness a light
That shines forth in your praise.
    And you stir from within
    Surrounding all life
    With your love.

In the breaking of bread,
The outpouring of wine
Event filled with Christ's presence
At table among us.

Engulfed, beheld, held are we
In your promise of life yet with us.
  And you stir from within
  Surrounding all life
  With your love.

As vessels of earth receiving of you
We are filled with new life
Beyond limit of death.
If broken, not crushed
Christ living in us.
Your glory revealed in great light.
  And you stir from within
  Surrounding all life
  With your love.

Grounded are we,
Rooted, called forth
By your Spirit within
To gather in trust of the impulse
Creative and moving without
To the ends of the earth sing your praise.

*Donna Kilarski is
campus minister at
Augustana
University College,
in Camrose, Alta.*

Magnificat

L'autre Parole Collectif

Mon âme exalte le Seigneur
et mon esprit s'est rempli d'allégresse
parce que les voix silencieuses d'hier
commencent à prendre la Parole.

Oui, désormais, les générations de femmes
s'engageront comme partenaires à part entière
dans l'Église comme dans la société

Les femmes proclameront leur foi, leur espérance et leur sacerdoce
afin que de générations en générations
en communion avec le Christ
s'accomplisse la libération de toutes les opprimées.

> Mon âme exalte le Seigneur,
> Exulte mon esprit.

> Car Dieu comme une Mère
> Console, relève, accompagne, accueille et garde
> Dans son sein toute sa création.

> Car des femmes aliénées
> Ont trouvé le chemin de l'autonomie.
> Des femmes écrasées
> Ont repris courage.

> Des femmes bafouées
> Ont relevé la tête

Selon la promesse fait à Isaie:
    "Ne crains pas, tu ne seras pas confondue.
    N'aie pas honte, tu n'auras plus à rougir."
Désormais;
Fils et fille crieront "Libération."

Mon âme glorifie le Seigneur
Parce qu'il m'a fait comprendre de grandes choses.
Il m'a révélé un aspect de lui-même
Grandement occulté depuis des siècles.
Désormais, je me sens bien née,
Fille de Dieu qui reflète son image,
Fière, autonome et pleine de joie,
Je veux oeuvrer dans la sororité
A l'avènement de la nouvelle humanité.

Il m'a désirée, m'a voulue femme.
Il m'a donné d'en pressentir le mystère,
Mystère de la vie enfouie dans ma chair.
Il m'a tracé la voie, m'a fait cheminer
Avec une multitude de femmes fécondées
Porteuses de vie
Mais pourtant harassées, accablées;
Avec elles, j'ai cru à sa promesse de libération
Car il comble de biens les affamés
Il élève les humbles, les enracinés dans la chair.
Il disperse les superbes, les assoiffés de pouvoir, d'idéologies et de
systèmes.

Il détrône les puissants et les orgueilleux
    qui se cachent derrière le rempart du discours officiel
        derrière l'opacité de la vérité acquise
        derrière l'épaisseur de l'image à protéger.
Il se souvient de son amour
Car son Verbe s'est fait chair.

Mon âme exalte la lumière
Qui illumine les coeurs remplis de tendresse.

Que soient proclamées bienheureuses
    celles qui, d'âge en âge, ont façonné
    la complicité, la sororité des femmes.

La sagesse dispersera les mâles à la pensée orgueilleuse
    et jettera les machos à bas de leurs trônes.

Les soeurs, les filles, les femmes,
    les amantes, les épouses, les sorcières
    seront réunies dans la joie et l'allégresse,
Et toute la violence mâle se retournera
    contre les hommes au coeur dur.

L'esprit de la tempête s'apaisera
    quand la justice triomphera
    et fera éclore nos fécondités nouvelles.

Anti-poverty rally,
Vancouver.

Reflections on the Edge

Carol Kilby

Based on Mark 5:21-34 and Luke 8:43-49

> *And when Jesus had crossed again in the boat to the other side, a great crowd gathered about him; and he was beside the sea.*

Sitting on the pine-scented shore of this northern Ontario lake, my private retreat, I imagine another shore: the stony beach and lush palms of Galilee. In the gulls' salute to the promise of a new day I hear the excited cries of recognition from those men and women who made their living fishing there.

In the gnarled and twisted pines leaning out over the lake I see the ill and the lame grasping for life in the healing sulphuric springs off that shore near Tiberius. The air is steamy, pungent with the odour of rotting wood, fish, and human flesh.

> *And there was a woman who had had a flow of blood for twelve years, who had suffered much under many physicians and had spent all that she had and was no better but rather grew worse.*

Relentless waves crowd me back, stirring the sands of unconsciousness and raising the stench of powerlessness from hopes soured in poverty. I want to turn my back on her stooped form, bent and weak from the endless welfare battle for disability pensions and mother's allowance. If I don't listen, her pleas for subsidized day care won't touch me. The sun's rays absorb the mist and dance on the water;

gazing into the reflection of a thousand mirrors, I see her....

She came up behind him and touched the fringe of his garment.

I see her, society's untouchable, grasp at the untouchable — the sacred tassels, reminders of all the commandments of the Torah, by tradition tied since the time of Moses on the four corners of a male garment.

I see her, the unclean woman, for centuries forbidden to touch the Torah, grasping at the healing powers of the scripture. I see her grasp at the personhood of God.

And immediately the flow of blood ceased. "Someone touched me; for I perceive that power has gone forth from me." And when the woman saw that she was not hidden, she came trembling, and falling down before him declared in the presence of all the people why she had touched him and how she had been healed. And he said to her, "Daughter, your faith has made you well; go in peace."

The cold waters awaken me to the miracle of the woman's inner power. A loon laughs and plunges into the lake to feed. I am immersed in memories of life as a single mother on the edge of a budget too small for housing, food, and church offerings.

Over me washes the familiar wave of panic — my fragile security swept away when tenants left, some taking my clothes, others my dignity. I ride the old wave of delight — bargains found in damaged cans and day-old bread.

I see afresh the blue of water and sky. I reach to embrace the newness of the day, of comfort, wholeness, and acceptable status regained in second marriage.

I strain to touch again the other side — poverty, distant now, but for many only a man away. I stretch to the realization that in the reaching I, too, can overcome powerlessness. I can touch the power of that woman on the other side, she whom society named unclean, whom Jesus called faithful and well.

In the lake's reflection I see my power is in the shimmering image of hands reaching past the edge of my existence, risking to touch the personhood of God in the midst of the single women, mothers, widows, and Native women, today's "daughters of Jerusalem."

I turn again, hands stretched out before me, to the clamouring crowds of the city, able now to look on its impoverished and feminine face without being drowned by the waves of powerlessness.

Carol Kilby
is a minister at
Eastminster United
Church, Toronto.

Woman and washing, Trout River, Nfld.

Where There Is No Vision, the Women Perish

Emma Marsh

O God! What's going to happen to me?
How many days has it been?
Six, I think, since my man fell on the floor.
Three sons in their bunks,
Their eyes never blink.
All dead, dead and gone.... Only me left,
me and the dogs.... The dogs, howling and
scratching at the porch door. Good thing, too,
for the thin hole they've made lets some snow in
for me to get a drink. They must be starving.
So am I.

O God, I'm so scared.... How long it's been since the
sickness struck. First one. Then the other.
Now I'm the only one left....
Funny how it took the strongest ones first.

It's getting dark again. Oh, I hate the nights!
The wind, the dogs, the shapes ... the shapes dancing
on the wall. Sometimes it looks like the boys are moving.
I'm so cold, but I suppose that's even better for the boys....
I'm so afraid. I'm so lonely.

How can I stay alive? Do I want to?
God, you have kept me alive. Why? Tell me, why?

I think I'm going mad ... just like the dogs!
Father, into thy ...

What's that racket? Frost cracking? Am I dying? Gunshots!
They're pushing the door open!
Mr. Gordon! Thank God you've come.

Aunt Liz Williams had survived for at least three weeks in a lonely house at North River, Labrador, before the missionary, Henry Gordon, found her. Her husband and three adult family members had died of the Spanish flu. Their bodies were in the cabin. She had had nothing to eat but dried flour. She obtained enough water to stay alive from the snow she melted by holding it close to her body.

Mr. Gordon took her to Cartwright, where, despite being seventy-five years of age, she recovered and helped care for children orphaned by the epidemic.

Yahweh! How bitter it was to leave Bethlehem, the house of bread, which had no bread! How bitter to be in the land of the heathen! Yet the bitterness could not touch the heart. The pain was absorbed in the love of a strong and good husband, Elimelech, with whom I could stand against the world.

His slow death brought a new bitterness.
Then our firstborn went down.
Then the youngest, the dreamer.
They are gone.

They are dead.

Do not call me Naomi, pleasantness. Call me Marah, bitterness.

Their wives are alive.

I love Orpah and Ruth too much to bring them to dwell with bitterness in Bethlehem.

But you, Yahweh, are with me. You must dwell with bitterness.

Will you absorb the bitterness?

Can I stand with you against the world?

> *Elimelech, the husband of Naomi, died, and she was left with her two sons. These took Moabite wives; the name of the one was Orpah and the name of the other Ruth. They lived there about ten years; and both Mahlon and Chilion died, so the woman was bereft of her two sons and her husband.*
>
> Ruth 1:3-5

In the face of overwhelming pain, struggle, and sorrow, we meet these two women. Both were women of faith who spoke often with God. Naomi and Aunt Liz had a vision of a God who was with them in good times and in bad. It was because of their vision of a God who shared their suffering that they not only survived but triumphed in the face of adversity.

Where there is no vision, the women perish.

Emma Marsh of Gander, Nfld., is a homemaker and expectant grandmother who has been a volunteer in church women's work for fifty years.

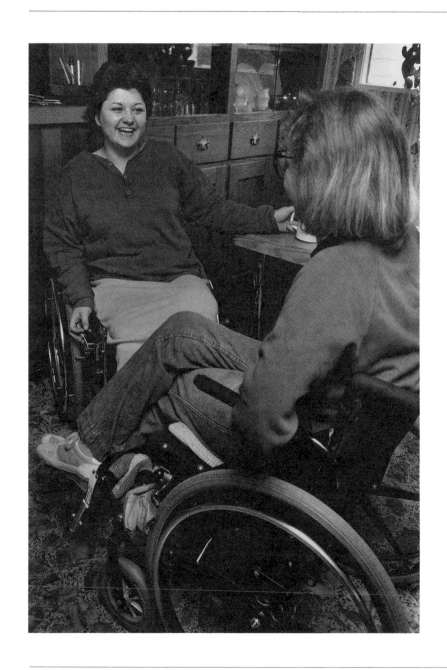

Judy Ryan
and Pat Danforth,
Dis-Abled Women's
Network (DAWN),
Regina, Sask.

Good News for Modern Woman

Lois Klempa

In recent years we have heard a great deal about women and the Bible —
too much, some may think. But many of us, particularly women, have in
a manner of speaking rediscovered the Bible. We have been startled to find
new meaning given to old passages, things formerly hidden, now revealed. Like buried treasure, scholars have unearthed passages for us that
have completely changed our understanding of what we believed God
was saying to women through the Word. It is like a gospel within the
gospel, truly "Good News for Modern Woman."

What has brought about this change? I think it can be attributed, at
least in part, to a new way of looking at scripture. We often make the Bible
say what we want it to say. We look for confirmation of our prejudices in
the Bible, and we usually find it. We must let the Bible speak for itself. We
must come to the Bible with an open mind, leaving behind our precon-
ceived ideas. We are so used to hearing the Bible interpreted from a
particular slant that, having ears to hear, we do not hear, and having eyes
to see, we do not see what the Holy Spirit is saying through the Word.

Isn't it curious that, throughout all these centuries, the church has
depended mainly on some advice given by Paul to the congregation at
Corinth for its teaching about the place of women, along with some
passages in Timothy attributed to him? As Leonard Swidler has commented in *Biblical Affirmations of Women*, "The restrictive statements concerning women in the Pauline and Petrine writings often were much more
influential than the very liberal statements and actions of Jesus concerning
women."[1]

Could that be because these passages verified what was already
believed about women? So these passages were emphasized, while

others, in which Paul refers to women as co-workers and partners in the gospel, were downplayed, along with his magnificent statement, "There is neither Jew nor Greek, bond nor free, male nor female, but all are one in Christ" (Gal. 3:28).

Women have been "slow of heart to believe," but the scales are gradually falling from our eyes, and we are beginning to see. And we wonder why we were so blind. How could we have read our Bible and missed what was so obvious? Why did we never before notice that Jesus' treatment of women was absolutely revolutionary, not just for his day, but for ours as well? Jesus went out of his way to make it abundantly clear that his teaching, unlike that of other rabbis, was meant for women as well as men. Search as you will, nowhere in any of the gospels will you find a word that would give any indication that Jesus believed women to be inferior or subordinate. No wonder women flocked to hear him. "Is it any wonder," as Dorothy Sayers says in *Are Women Human*, that women "were first at the cradle and last at the cross? They had never known a man like this Man — there has never been such another...."[2]

We can no longer ignore the biblical testimony that female disciples were with Jesus from the beginning of his ministry in Galilee, travelling with him and the male disciples; that it was to the woman of Samaria that Jesus first revealed himself as Messiah; that it was to Martha that Jesus said, "I am the Resurrection and the Life" (John 11:25; Matt. 16:16), and that her confession, "You are the Christ," matches that of Peter's "Great Confession."

Only in recent years have we been bold enough to proclaim the amazing testimony of all the gospels that Jesus appeared first to Mary Magdalene and the other women and it was to them that Christ first gave the commission, "Go and tell my brothers," causing later writers to refer to Mary as "the apostle to the apostles."

We have made assumptions: for example, that the two disciples on the road to Emmaus (Luke 24:13-25) were both men, when the Greek text (and most translations) do not identify Cleopas' companion. Does it make sense to believe that two men, rather than a wife and husband, would be going home and inviting Jesus to eat with them, particularly when Cleopas is likely the "Clopas" mentioned in John 19:25, whose wife Mary was one of the women at the cross?

In this Decade of the Churches in Solidarity with Women, I think it would be well for us to attend to the words of Katherine Bushnell, a scholar of Hebrew and Greek, from her book *God's Word to Women,* written in 1924 and recently reprinted:

> "In the study of God's messages to women, I wish you to approach His Book as though ... you had never seen it before and knew nothing about it. Will you endeavour to cultivate this spirit of fresh inquiry? When we have heard over and over again, with unquestioning credulity, an explanation of a thing, even though the explanation be grotesque, it comes back to us with all the force of natural fact.... If there be an error in the explanation, we arrive at a point where we can detect it only by a real effort; the false view comes to mind first, and hinders acceptance of the true."[3]

1. Leonard Swidler, *Biblical Affirmations of Women* (Philadelphia: The Westminster Press, 1969), 162.
2. Dorothy Sayers, *A Matter of Eternity/Are Women Human?* (Grand Rapids, Mich.; Eerdmans, 1973), 47.
3. Katherine C. Bushnell, *God's Word to Women* (Jacksonville, Fla.; Ray B. Munson) unpaged, lesson 3.

Lois Klempa of Westmount, Que., is a graduate of Ewart College, Toronto, and has served on several boards and committees of the Presbyterian Church in Canada.

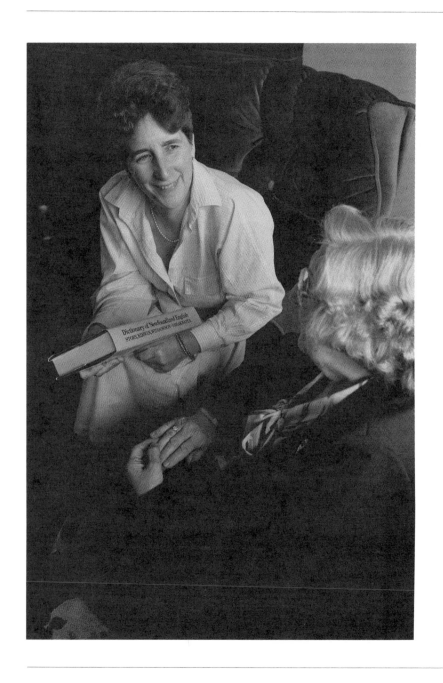

Sheila Drover and her mother, Margaret McKinnon, Cornerbrook, Nfld.

I Am No Longer Afraid

Julia Esquivel
(adapted by Linnea Good)

I am no longer afraid of death.
I know too closely its cold, dark corridors.
I am no longer afraid of death.
I know these caverns that lead to life.

I am afraid of a life of dying,
A life that hasn't passed through death,
That cramps our hands and slows our marching,
That sings the songs of borrowed breath.

But I am no longer afraid of death.
I know too closely its cold, dark corridors.
I am no longer afraid of death.
I know these caverns that lead to life.

I am afraid of the fear within me,
And other's fear that digs their grave,
Who cling to ways that whisper healing,
But lead a road that cannot save.

But I am no longer afraid of death.
I know too closely its cold, dark corridors.
I am no longer afraid of death.
I know these caverns that lead to life.

I live each day to kill our death.
I die each day to beget our living.
And in this dying unto death,
I am reborn, my hope's full giving.

But I am no longer afraid of death.
I know too closely its cold, dark corridors.
I am no longer afraid of death.
I know these caverns that lead to life.

Music for this song is available in *There Is a Time,* by Linnea Good and Friends, 258 Church St., Fredericton, NB E8B 4E4.

*Julia Esquivel
is a Guatemalan
Presbyterian pastor
and poet in exile.
Linnea Good, who
wrote the song based
on her poem, is a
Vancouver composer
and musician.*

Sunset at Netsilik
River Camp, near
Spence Bay, N.W.T.

Tabitha

Gail Golding

Based on John 7:53-8:11

My name is Tabitha. I am the woman whom men brought to Jesus, humiliated and disgraced. They said I should be stoned. They said they had caught me "in the very act of adultery." I am so confused....I didn't mean to do anything so awful.

When I was a young girl, I fell in love. My life revolved around my lover; my spirits rose and fell with his coming and going. I was proud to be with him. Everyone spoke well of him. When he asked me to marry him, my heart nearly burst with joy.

But he is no longer pleased with me. He calls me ugly names and swears at me when I ask for money to buy food for the children. He no longer touches me gently. Mostly, he doesn't touch me at all. When he does, it is rough and demanding and over quickly.

But I long to share my life with a man. My soul longs for a man's love; my spirit, for a man's companionship; my body, for a man's strong and gentle touch. Yesterday, I felt so empty and alone. When my little boy disobeyed, I lost control and left bruises on his back. Afterward, I cried and cried.

Last evening, the man at the market said my eyes were sad; he gave me a treat he had saved for the children. Then he asked me to meet him down by the shore behind the rocks. I never did anything like that before; but I was so happy that he wanted to be with me!

Then the men came. They shouted and grabbed me and dragged me across the rocks. See, here are the scrapes and bruises. But they didn't do anything to the man from the market. He didn't do anything to stop them, either. He just sat there and watched them drag me away.

The men took me to the authorities. The authorities took me to Jesus. I heard them talking among themselves. They wanted to trick him, but when he spoke, they all disappeared. I was so embarrassed.... I didn't want to look at him ... and then ... he spoke to me!

He wasn't like my husband or the man from the market or the other men. His eyes were so gentle and sad. I thought he hurt as much as me. It seemed as though he knew all about me ... and somehow that made it okay. I wonder if he knows what I did to my little boy.

There is something unusual.... I don't know.... I wonder ... if I keep my mind on his eyes, could it help me not to hurt my children? Could it help me stand the loneliness?

Gail Golding of Halifax is a candidate for diaconal ministry who has been involved for a number of years in issues related to family violence.

Who Sinned?

Karen Dukes

Jesus looked up and said to her, "Woman, where are they? Has no one condemned you?" She said, "No one, Lord." And Jesus said, "Neither do I condemn you; go, and do not sin again."

John 8:10-11

No one ever looked at me the way Billy does. His eyes light up.

My husband? Moose hunting — or duck, or deer.

I forget which.

When Billy saw the cut on my mouth he went white. Reached out his finger so gently, like a butterfly. His kiss so light I could hardly feel it. "I'll kill him," he said.

Ma drank. Daddy swore at her and slapped her around, then he'd get that funny smile and come for me.

Sixteen when I left, God. He promised he'd look after me.

The bruises don't hurt so much. It's the names: lazy, stupid, slut, crazy bitch.

What if he's right?

Just talking to Billy made me feel like gold and diamonds, like sunshine and sky. Would you know about that, God? He made me feel light and pretty and clean. I didn't know I could feel that way, just knew I felt safe and good with Billy. Safe! Have you ever needed to feel safe, God?

It's the rules, isn't it? Is it the rules that matter to you, God? Have you got all this down somewhere in your book, black marks against me?

He doesn't hit me often, not every day. He buys the food and pays the bills. Got me a pretty sweater once. If only he'd take his ring off first....

I'll try, I'll try harder, please stop....

Billy cried when he saw the stitches, held me and shook all over. He says I should leave.

It's a sin, right, God? I'm trying to be good. He comes home tomorrow. Oh, God, what will I do?

I guess it doesn't matter much. If I wasn't bad already you wouldn't let him beat me. Would you, God? Maybe you can't stop him either. After all, they beat you, too.

I'm going, God. Billy and I are going to Vancouver. He's got work there. He says I can go back to school, make something of myself. He believes I can do it. I'm going to try. Thanks for listening.... See you around, God.

But God, who sinned?

*Karen Dukes
is an Anglican
parish priest in
Cardinal, Ont.*

Women's Support Group, Crowbush, P.E.I.

En Mémoire D'elles

Denyse Joubert-Nantel

Nos émouvantes chimères
se sont changées, hier,
en larmes amères.

Nous, filles, épouses, mères,
célébrons, ce soir, ce mémorial
de la violence ancestrale
issue de profondeurs viscérales.

Répons: En mémoire d'elles

Du Levant au Ponant
du magistère à l'Iman,
soumises aux interdits infamants,
suppliciées dans notre chair: pieds sanglés,
sexe couturé, cous et lèvres disloqués.

Répons: En mémoire d'elles

Odalisque ou châtelaine ceinturée,
Droit de cuissage arrogé,
Sorcières brûlées,
Inceste, viol, violences subtilement voilées.

Répons: En mémoire d'elles

Mineures par Napoléon codées,
Salariées exploitées,
Pauvreté féminisée,
Sages-femmes ostracisées,
Droit de vie criminalisé,
Droit de vote nié,
Pornographie vidéoclipée,
Publicité sexisée rétrogradée,
Et que de chaînes de sévices innommés ...

Ministère inaccessibilisé,
Postes cadres, chasse gardée

Répons: En mémoire d'elles

(Chacune est invitée à nommer une violence qu'elle a subie. Chaque intervention est suivie du répons.)

Notre tumulte émotionnel se morcelant dans le noir,
Que d'interrogations nous habitent, ce soir!...
Notre peine indicible, nos gémissements, nos hurlements
Questionnent, de la société, les comportements.

Ô victimes innocentes d'une sauvage loterie,
Fauchées à l'Aurore d'une vie de "bâtisseuses-égéries,"
Que vos assises sanglantes ne se terrent pas dans le noir:
Qu'elles rayonnent, nouveau REPOSOIR,
La Justice et irradient nos espoirs.

Extrait du déroulement d'une célébration par le groupe Vasthi sur le drame de l'École Polytechnique.

Denyse Joubert-Nantel est poétesse et membre de L'autre Parole collectif, Montréal.

Drink Deeply

Karen Weatherington

Drink deeply, oh my sister, of the pain that you feel.
Draw strength from your tears;
Let the hurt begin to heal.

Reach out, oh my sister, to the light that is here.
Be strong in your aloneness;
Don't give in to the fear.

For I know that in the morning, when the dark is cast away,
We will dance with joy and singing for the hope of this new day.
We will rejoice in God, our Mother, who brings life out of decay,
For our strength is in the knowing we are growing in new ways.
We will rejoice in God, our Mother, who brings life out of decay,
For our strength is in the knowing we are growing in new ways.

DRINK DEEPLY

Words & Music by
Karen Weatherington

1. Drink deep-ly, oh my sis-ter, of the pain that you feel. Draw
2. Reach out, oh my sis-ter, to the light that is here. Be

strength from your tears; let the hurt be-gin to heal.
strong in your a-lone-ness; don't give in to the fear.

With Joy

3. For I know that in the morn-ing, when the dark is cast a-

-way, we will dance with joy and sing-ing for the hope of this new

day. We will re - joice in God, our Moth-er, who brings life out of de-

-cay, for our strength is in the know-ing we are grow - ing in new

ways. We will re - joice in God, our Moth - er, who brings

life out of de - cay, for our strength is in the

know-ing we are grow - ing in new ways.

*Karen
Weatherington
is a music student
at Augustana
University College
in Camrose, Alta.*

47

*Mrs. Parsons
in her kitchen,
Trout River, Nfld.*

A Woman's Defiant Lament

Janet Silman

Scripture reading: Judges 4

O Canada, our home and native land,
what have you done
where are our leaders
silent, washing their hands, on holiday
while Native elders, women and children
run the gauntlet of white mobs
stoning their cars with rocks
the time is past to talk of shades of grey
of white men's moral ambiguities
when brown flesh and red blood are facing down
the barrels of four thousand soldiers' guns
O Canada, this is our Wounded Knee
our own deep south and ghetto civil war
our David and Goliath just begun
and though I may hate guns
I reaffirm my commitment
to the cause of Native rights and land
to the Spirit of love and justice and peace
I lament for you, O Canada
for the shame of your pale, weak pharaohs
who do not know the strength of dreams
the power of a people who see
their hope is stronger than death
and stronger than one day's defeat.

Oka women
I was so proud when you strode
between the soldiers and your warriors
who were screaming, guns raised
adrenalin pumping rage and fear
ready to kill
you took control
you grabbed your frenzied warrior
dangerously close to drawing fire
you pushed him back
screamed orders at your brothers
commands they obeyed
while television eyes watched amazed
at your power and take-charge bravery
I was so proud of you, Mohawk women
you reminded me of those strong Hebrew women
Miriam and Hagar, Deborah and Jael
women who stood their ground for their people
Oka women, Hebrew women, strong women
may your powerful spirit infuse our times.
O Source of all creative power
infuse us with courage
Creator Spirit, lead us to justice and peace.

Written on Labour Day, 1990, during the last stand of the Mohawk warriors, women, and
children at Oka, in their conflict with the government of Quebec over sacred land.

*Janet Silman is on
the staff of the
Manitoba and
Northwestern
Ontario Conference
of the United
Church.*

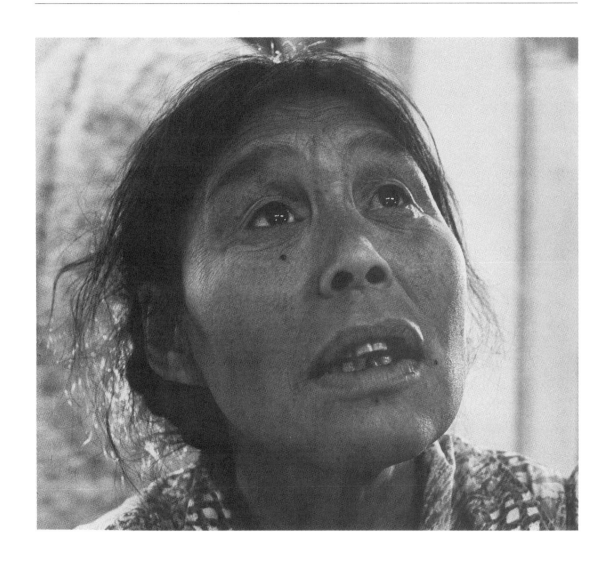

Craftswoman,
Spence Bay, N.W.T.

Ballade des Exilées

Marie Gratton Boucher

Psaume pour un temps de disgrâce, inspirée du psaume 137

Au bord des fleuves de tous les exils
auxquels nous condamne le patriarcat,
nous nous tenons debout,
le temps n'est plus aux larmes,
aux peupliers d'alentour
reste hissée la bannière de nos combats.

Et c'est là que nos geôliers osent
nous demander des cantiques,
les ravisseurs de notre liberté chrétienne
nous commander des chants de joie.
"Chantez-nous, disent-ils,
un cantique de soumission,
là seulement vous trouverez
votre salut et votre gloire."

Comment chanterions-nous
un cantique à l'Esprit qui libère
sur une terre où l'on nous traite en étrangères?
Si je t'oublie, liberté chrétienne,
Que ma droite ... et ma gauche se dessèchent!

Que ma langue s'attache à mon palais
si je perds ton souvenir,
toi qui fraternisas avec Jeanne,
Salomé, Marthe, Marie et la Samaritaine.
Mourront mes soeurs et mes filles,
mes frères et mes fils,
emportés par un même malentendu,
si je ne mets pas ton message libérateur
au plus haut de ma joie!

Souviens-toi de nous,
inaugurateur de la nouvelle Alliance,
contre les défenseurs et les détenteurs
du pouvoir patriarcal
que perpétue ton Église.

Souviens-toi de nous quand ils disent:
"Femmes, vous n'avez pas de place parmi nous,
tenez-vous à l'écart, restez soumises.
Quel autre honneur vous faut-il?
Comme soeurs, comme mères, comme servantes,
mésestimeriez-vous, ingrates, le privilège
d'être l'escabeau de nos pieds?"

Patriarcat dévastateur,
nous n'appelons pas contre toi le feu du ciel,
déjà tu trembles sur tes bases,
nous ne souhaitons pas que tu paies davantage
le prix des maux que tu nous valus.
Heureux cependant qui saisira les signes des temps
et brisera les jougs qui nous oppriment,
qui pavera la voie pour le retour des exilées.
Heureux les hommes de bonne volonté
prisonniers eux aussi de la forteresse patriarcale
qui souhaitent remiser les trônes,
descendre les ponts-levis et combler les fossés.

Au bord des fleuves de tous les exils,
nous nous tenons debout,
le temps n'est plus aux larmes,
(peut-être n'est-il même plus aux revendications).

Au bord des fleuves de tous les exils,
fortes de ta mémoire, fils de Marie,
pour la justice,
nous bâtissons!

Marie Gratton Boucher est professeure de théologie à l'Université de Sherbrooke.

Ownership

ruby reske-naurocki

how can you buy or sell the warmth of the land
the idea was strange to my Native sister
the elders had taught her
that they were one with the land
and the land was one with them
the land was sacred to her and her people
for thousands of years
they had lived in peace on the land
in reverence of its quiet strength

ownership
the white man's way
what he cannot buy he takes
and everywhere the earth is sore
and her children are hungry

ownership
the white man's lie
each generation pays for the same piece of land
every bank gets fat on the interest
and forty thousand children die each day
from hunger
such trickery
sucks life from the land
and shackles the soul

we were not made to be serfs
we are called to be stewards
for we are part of the land
of the Spirit of the land
we cannot own anything
for everything is a gift
and the Spirit that made us
is with us
waiting for us
to awaken from our sleep
to empower us with strong gentleness
to experience the bounties of the land
the peace and justice meant for us

awake then
the big sleep is over
arise and go forth in faith
for life is like the flash of a firefly
let us burn brightly
our time is now
and be not afraid
for as my sister sings
all that we own is our soul
and all things are possible with the Spirit
that does not sleep

ruby reske-naurocki
farms in the
Beausejour, Man.,
area and is an
active member
of the National
Farmers Union.

Jane Morrison,
dairy farmer,
Scotsburn, N.S.

The Promise of Justice

H. Miriam Ross

Scripture reading: Isaiah 42:1-4; Matthew 12:18-21

A bruised reed he will not break and a dimly burning wick he will not quench; he will faithfully bring forth justice.

Isaiah 42:3 (*NRSV*)

In a world where justice, gentleness, and faithfulness are in short supply, the servant songs of Isaiah ring with assurance and hope. The prophet uses common household objects familiar to Hebrew women to illustrate the tender care that marks the character of the servant.

In ancient Israel, reeds or flowering stalks from various kinds of tall marsh grasses were used for thatching houses, for measuring lengths, and for separating threads on the weaver's loom. Weak and fragile, these wild grasses had to be handled carefully if they were to serve useful functions. They could easily be brushed aside, trampled underfoot, totally crushed.

Isaiah speaks of a reed that has been bruised. The servant is aware of its presence. He could easily snap off the stalk, grind out its life. Instead, the servant handles the reed with great care to prevent further damage and to stimulate its life forces.

As women, we can find solace in such solicitude. How often have we felt weak, fragile, defenceless, on the verge of extinction? How often have we been ignored, put down, rejected, damaged by abuse or rape or incest, overwhelmed by family responsibilities or poverty? Isaiah brings us good news. Rather than adding to our humiliation, the servant comes to us to offer strength and hope.

Another homey illustration reinforces this image of the caring servant. Fibres from dried stalks of the flax plant were separated, then combed and spun into thread for linen cloth. The fibres were also used to make slow-burning wicks for lamps. If the oil were low or the wick not properly trimmed, the flame would smoulder and smoke, producing an acrid odour and a feeble, flickering light. Isaiah illustrates the patience of the servant who refrains from snuffing out this faltering, ineffective lamp.

Again, women can enter into the illustration as we admit our tendency to be passive, to wait for others to direct us, to leave our talents dormant in our fear of the cost of cultivating and taking responsibility for them. Just as a smouldering wick does not fulfil its function, we often do not carry out the things of which we are capable. Behind a smiling facade, we bear the burden of resentment and anger; and as the years go by, we may find ourselves in a crisis of faith.

But Isaiah sets out the promise. The servant will not snuff out a smouldering wick; instead, he fans the flickering flame until it again spreads light. We, too, can take heart; the servant knows and respects us even at the low points of our lives when we feel useless and forsaken. He is there to help us review our situation, to reassess our alternatives, to look for different resources, and to rebound in faith and hope. Change is possible because the servant is determined to respond to the despairing cry of the downtrodden, to plead and defend our case until justice is established.

Matthew 12:20 applies this prophecy to the work of Jesus, who healed the sick, fed the hungry, and stood for the poor and deprived against the religious leaders of his day. Instead of death, he brought life, for he was committed to justice and conferred release and relief, hope and blessing.

The Spirit empowers us today to work together to loosen bonds, to strengthen those who have been crushed like broken reeds and to fan gently into flame the life forces of those nearly burned out by violence and despair.

*Dr. H. Miriam Ross
is associate
professor of
Christian missions
and social issues
at Acadia
Divinity College,
Wolfville, N.S.*

Roots and Wings

Linnea Good

Tie me down, roots and wings
flow through my branches, the life of the earth.
Teach me the ancient songs of the soil.
Let me fly, roots and wings
high through the mountains,
along with the clouds,
follow my dreams as they fly.
For with water and bread,
the sun and the air,
we need roots for the ground
and wings for the sky.

Spirit of rain be my parent.
Spirit of snow be my child.
I am the oak with her roots pushing strong.
I am the swallow with flight in her song.
I am rooted, yet soar in the wild.

Shall you find one for a lover?
Why might you ask them to stay?
Will they know the deep pushing roots of your soul?
Will theirs wrap around them as seasons grow old?
Will you both find your wings know the way?

What shall we bring as our off'ring?
With what shall we come to the day?
The song of the ancients, the desert, the field,
The song of the infants, the playground, the wheel.
In the dance of the ages we'll play.

How are you making your living?
Do you give back to the earth?
Have you given flight to the dreams that you keep?
Have you touched the underground streams of the deep?
Come, give your imaginings birth!

Music for this song is available in *There Is a Time,* by Linnea Good and Friends, 258 Church St., Fredericton, NB E8B 4E4.

Linnea Good is a
Vancouver composer
and musician.

*Bev Morrow,
farmer, Women
of Unifarm member,
Barrhead, Alta.*

Bear My Burden

Patricia Roberts

I hold my baby in my arms
And see his fragile face,
The memory of a sturdy child
I cannot quite erase.

I hold my baby in my arms.
There's famine in the land.
Dry winds blow dust and dirt around.
There's vermin in the sand.

I hold my baby in my arms.
Flies crawl across his cheek.
He needs both food and water now.
He seems so ill and weak.

You hold a baby in your arms.
His skin is bright and clear.
He moves his hands, he plays and laughs,
Bears a promise for each year.

I hold my baby in my arms,
And Jesus holds him too.
He calls out just one question:
Disciple, what will you do?

He holds my baby in his arms.
He wonders who will come
To bear my burden, bring relief,
And say, "Thy will be done."

Patricia Roberts is a concerned grandmother and active member in her parish, St. Mary's, Beaconsfield, Que.

*June Clark-
Greenberg,
Montreal.*

Spiral of Life

JoAnn Symonds

My heart speaks of former beliefs,
Embraced by a God of nature,
Centred on the sacred earth.
The green spiral of life begs for my return.
The small circle I was concerned with was so safe,
I chose only that which I wanted to see.
Now my vision has broadened,
The white of naiveté has become a blinding light,
Exposing me to the reds of anger and purple,
Woman's unfair share.
Purple life spirals,
Searching for ways to remove stones,
Looking for rainbows, symbols of hope.
And then there is space,
Spirit space, where the breath of God transforms,
Allowing diversive thinking.
Space to move in;
Space to change in;
Space to grow in;
There must always be space!

*JoAnn Symonds of
St. Albert, Alta.,
is a nurse and a
theology student
at St. Stephen's
College, Edmonton.*

So You've Been Asked to Lead!

Charlotte Caron

God of all people, share with us in our common life.
Give us grace to listen as we lead.
Help us to share leadership and power with all whose lives are affected
by our work, and to value the wisdom that resides in us and in others
so that justice may reign.
Give us courage to lead when it is our turn,
to step aside when it is time to do so,
to risk for the cause of love and life,
to laugh when there is joy and weep when there is sorrow.
Whether we lead in the context of our own homes and with our
children,
in the church or women's group of which we are a part,
or in the public arena, in organizations or politics,
help us to use the inner resources we have and to value the gifts of
others to bring about goodness for all.
We offer this prayer trusting in you, O God, and in ourselves.
Amen.

*Charlotte Caron
is on the staff of
St. Andrew's
College, Saskatoon.*

Images of Myself

JoAnne M. Walter

There is no part of me unlovely
    Not the anger, or the pain, or the sorrow,
Not this physical being others see as me.
These are the things that draw me deeper
    into womanhood
    where I am called to be.
It is the place where we have met,
    To grieve and laugh and celebrate.

My conception was not a loving act.
    Yet I was born in love.
Born in the valley of the Bow
In the shadow of the rugged Rocky Mountains
Urged in my birthing by the icy
    swiftness of that river,
Cradled by the fragrant earth and pines,
Tuned to the heartbeat of all Time.

From the depths of emerald lakes
    my image comes to me
Reflecting what I see and know as part of me.
I feel the purity of living streams
    flow through my veins.
I touch the crystal dew drops on the leaves,
    akin to those that draw you into me.

I hear the thunder of the waterfall
    repeated in the pounding of my heart.
Like the mountains I brood and stand aloof,
And hide my secrets in the dark.

Born a woman
I hear the travail of the earth,
The inner weeping for the desecration,
The pain of widows, still in mourning
The loneliness of lovers when dreams have died.
    This life I live is mine
But it's been home to others.
Love has buried treasures
    in my soul
Shared with those who listen
    to the silence of the mountains.

*JoAnne M. Walter
is a deaconess and
hospital visitor
born in Calgary,
who currently lives
in Stoney Creek,
Ont.*

Leavings

Beth Sewell

Life is a leaving.

A baby leaves the womb
    Torn apart ... separated ...
        Thrust into newness.

A child leaves the nursery
    Timid ... insecure ...
        Pushed into competition.

A girl leaves her parents
    Starry-eyed ... glowing ...
        Romanced into marriage.

A woman leaves her yesterdays
    Fearful ... alone ...
        Forced into tomorrow.

And me? I leave
    My youth ... my role ...
        My "me"
    Awakened into self.

*Beth Sewell
is the pseudonym
of an Ontario
churchwoman.*

Creator, Parent, Spirit God

Jean Munro Gordon

Creator God
When I think of you, I marvel at
the vastness of the universe,
    the complexities of humanity,
    the intricacies of all life forms.
As I make bread
I relate to you as
    provider, Creator.
In countless ways I experience your creativity:
    in my new granddaughter ...
    in the love of my family ...
    in friends of varying colour and culture.
For your creation and creativity,
For your energetic activity in all of life,
Thank you, Creator God.

Parent God,
Because I didn't know my father,
I cannot worship you as a father figure.
When I was young, the presence of my friends' fathers
    made me uncomfortable.
But, Father God,
I recall the strong arms of a man
    who carried me, at the early age of four,
    over a dangerous bridge.
It helped me to know you as Father.
When our children were born,

the love and protection of their father, my husband,
　　showed me a loving father.
My son, a new father, has experienced that kind of love.
He says, "I didn't know I could love so much."
Thank you, Father God.
But I recall the screams of my mother,
　　and the blood
　　and my growing years without a father.
The concept of you as Father is still difficult.
Perhaps to image you as a mother figure is my need.
The injury of my mother's psyche
　　as she blamed herself
　　for marriage failure
affected her performance as a mother.
Yet love was there.
I, as a mother,
　　know the demands and expectations
　　a mother experiences:
　　　　the depths of joy,
　　　　the hopes and heartaches.
To know that these are yours too
　　affirms and comforts me.
Thank you, Mother God.

Parent God,
　　because I have experienced family and parenthood,
I can relate to you.
Thank you, Parent God.

Spirit God,
You dwell in me.
You are always present.
In my thinking and my being.
In hope and courage
    strength and power
    joy and grief
    peace and justice.
You are universal,
    in the wind that moves the nations toward peace ...
    in the blossom that delights ...
    in the child full of promise.
You come to me
    through friends and books ...
    in the compassionate Jesus ...
    in freedom to aid the powerless, the beaten, the poor,
    the discriminated against, the fearful.
You are liberator,
    that which is;
You are growth,
    that which is to be.

You are love in its broadest, highest, deepest, and inmost sense.
Thank you, Spirit God.

Creator God, Parent God, Spirit God,
    grow in me ...
    affirm me ...
    refine me ...
Amen.

Jean Munro Gordon is a past president of the Women's Inter-Church Council of Canada who lives in Milton, N.S.

*Katy Harris-McLeod
and her
grandmother,
Florence Harris,
having a tea party,
Creemore, Ont.*

Peeling

Donna Sinclair

I used to help my mother peel the apples
letting the skin peel down into a strip as long as
I could make it.

Now I peel the edges from computer paper.
Sometimes I try to see
how long
I can
make
the strip.
My daughter doesn't know about the apples.

*Donna Sinclair is a
writer from North
Bay, Ont.*

For Nancy

Donna Kilarski

Moonflower, daughter of youthfulness
    daughter of youthfulness
    woman of compassion and power,
You dance through us
    and move the deep knowing waters
    within.
As surely as at your birth
    a song was sung,
It resounds again,
Calling us to receive its gift
    and to celebrate the borning.

Donna Kilarski is campus minister at Augustana University College in Camrose, Alta.

A Meditation

Betty Turcott

Based on Isaiah 43:1

Sit comfortably and begin to quiet your body and mind.
Rest your feet firmly on the floor.
Fill the chair, feel it holding you.
Rest your hands comfortably in your lap.
Relax your shoulders.
If you wish, close your eyes.

Be aware of your breathing.
Don't alter it. Just be aware of it.
In and out. In and out.
Be aware of the calm and quiet in the room.
Be aware of your own presence in the room.

Recall the events of the past few days.
Remember the things you did this past week.
Remember something that didn't go as you had hoped.
Remember something you did well.

Recall some things that happened:
some things brought sadness ...
some things brought joy ...
some things brought a sense of completeness ...
some things are as yet unfinished....

Let us make an end to this time gone by.
Let us offer it to God, knowing that,
with its imperfections,
with its incompleteness,
it is accepted.
Just as each one of us is accepted.

Let us hear a word from Isaiah:
Fear not, for I have redeemed you; I have called you by name,
you are mine.

In your mind, say your name.
Repeat it two or three times.
Are there variations? A short form, a nickname?
Do you know what your name means?
Do you know why your name was chosen for you?

See your name printed.
See it in your own handwriting.

Hear it whispered gently.
Hear it spoken firmly.
Hear it shouted.
Was someone calling you?
Was your name called in anger?
Was it called in joy? excitement? fear?
Call your name out to the mountains.

Hear it echo ... echo ... echo ...
until you can't hear it any more.

Suggestions for use in group worship

The leader should have a calm and quiet voice, good reading skills and be well prepared. Call the group together and wait for quiet before you begin. Suggest that all papers, books, or purses be placed on the floor.

Direct the group by reading the meditation. Pause at the end of each phrase. At the end, ask them, when they are ready, to open their eyes and look around. Invite them to share with one other person anything they wish from the experience of the last few minutes. Then bring them together as a group to share anything that needs to be talked about.

Betty Turcott is a past president of the Women's Inter-Church Council of Canada and a hymn writer, who lives in Bowmanville, Ont.

Yvel Mazerolle, co-ordinator of Nouveau Départ in Moncton, N.B., and her son Julien.

In the Image of God

Rosemary Doran

> *So God created humankind in God's image; male and female God created them.*
>
> Adapted from Genesis 1:27

Among the most awesome moments of my life have been those times when, in turn, I held each of my newborn children in my arms and marvelled at the miracle of life, seeing stamped on each tiny face the family traits, the pattern of the generations.

In the years that followed, people would often look at my son or one of my daughters and exclaim, "You look so like your father," or "I can see your mother in you," for each one reflects something of my husband and me. To know us is to know something about our children. To know our children is to know something about us.

God created humankind in God's image.
To know ourselves, then, is to know something about God.
What can I know about God from myself?
I am human, I am woman.
I know joy and tenderness,
    patience and empathy,
    long-suffering and endurance,
    creativity and nurturing.
Are these not also found in God?

I am human, I am woman.
I know pain — physical and emotional —
and outrage
and frustration
and, sometimes, despair.
Does God not also know these?

I am human, I am woman.
My self-awareness enables my God-awareness, illuminates for me
what God is.

To know myself is to know something about God.
And to know God is also to know something about myself.
God not only is,
God also does,
therefore God's activity must be reflected in me.

Even as God speaks,
calls,
sends,
challenges,
loves,
So also must I, a human, a woman, made in God's image.

I must speak out about injustice,
call myself and others to responsibility,
send myself and others to serve,

challenge my family, my generation, my society to re-examine its values,
    love my neighbour — wherever, whoever, however he or she is.

Only then will the image of God in me be true, closer to perfection.
We are all God's children.
When I look at you, I am looking for God's image in you.
When you look at me, do you see that image in me?
God grant that I may reflect something of the one who brought me into being.

Rosemary Doran
is a minister
of Riverside
Presbyterian
Church,
Windsor, Ont.

Giigs (Grandmother)

Monica McKay

Giigs, my heart misses you.
My flesh and bones which clothe my soul
ache to hold you close to my heart.

Across all the miles that separate us, it is not
hard to join with you in mind's eye.

From our beginning we knew the power that was
given to the women of the Nisga'a nation. We are
Life-Givers, Life-Sustainers, providers, teachers;
within us is the power to re-create life.

I have heard the wisdom that you possess and know
that your wisdom is recognized and respected. You
stand as a matriarch within the house of Bil'.*

You know the property rights that our house has been blest with;
you know the names that belong to our house and as
caretaker you have never considered this your
right.

You are strong like the river, the river that
provides for us.

Like her, your strength is demonstrated by the
gentleness that comes from your very soul.
Yet the currents beneath the surface are like the
ideals you live your life by.

When the river is turbulent, you are angry because
someone has tried to hurt one of your family.
Your family is not the be all and end all
of you.
But that is not just you, it is all of us.
It is this way of life that you have instilled in
us.

If I look into the mirror I do not see my
reflection alone;
I see many who are my family, tribe ... my people.

But I am alone,
    look at me.

*The Nisga'a nation's social structure is based on a crest system. This is very much rooted
in their creation story. *House* not only describes a physical structure but the matrilineage,
the birthright inheritance coming from the mother.

*Monica McKay
is a member of the
Nisga'a first nation
in northwestern
British Columbia.*

*Patricia MacKay
and Judith Arbus
at a women's
celebration, Toronto.*

Come, Sing a Song

Anna Briggs

A hymn is a prayer-poem that becomes your own as you sing it. When we write hymns today that begin with "We" and address God as "You," we get away from the hymnody of Almighty-God-in-the-sky who saves (or damns) the individual soul, and we begin to talk to God as a community that understands that the mortal danger to our earth is caused by a sinful community indulging in communal greed and power seeking.

When I write hymns about creation or violence against women, about the anger and impatience we must have and use to change the world, or about gospel stories, I envisage them being sung in a church that is being transformed from hierarchy to community, from excluding to inclusive, from rules to freedom, a church that takes to its heart the pain and joy of women.

Here are two; I hope you will sing them and make them your own.

You Gave Us to Each Other
Suggested tune: "St. Flavian"

You gave us to each other, Lord,
In love to live and grow,
One flesh created, giving life,
Delight and trust to know.

With grace for joy and constancy
You bless each human soul,
To mirror your self-giving love,
Make mind and body whole.

But anguished cries now rise to you
From hearts betrayed and shamed,
By lashing tongue and thrusting fist,
And touch unasked, un-named.

The hands you made for tender care,
Love's openness to tell,
Strip self-esteem, wreak fear and death,
Make home a hidden hell.

Stretch out your nail-marked hands in love,
Make violence to cease,
Heal those whose cruel acts and words
Destroy their loved ones' peace.

Upturn the trade that thrives on force,
Deliver those in pain,
Bring justice, liberty from fear,
And hope to live again.

Let Our Anger Be a Blessing
Suggested tune: "Hyfrodol" or "Hymn to Joy"

Let our anger be a blessing,
Liberty for minds once numb;
Freedom from the old temptation
To indifference to succumb;

Take the energy it gives us,
Fire to build a world restored;
Overturn the changers' tables,
Cleanse our hearts to hear your word.

Lullaby

A note about this song (not a hymn). It was written in response to too many Advent sermons that see pregnancy as an ideal state, free from stigma, fear, pain, and foreboding. My Mary knows only too well what her pregnancy and motherhood may entail: disgrace and possible death, miscarriage, stillbirth, death from famine, disease, war, or violence for her child. It may be sung to the tune that follows it, which I wrote for my son Daniel, who died in 1985.

Stay, my child, my body sharing;
Girlhood's peace from me is torn;
Well I know a mother's fearing
Hope miscarried, joy stillborn;
    Lullaby, lullaby,
    God awaits a baby's cry,
    Lullaby.

Grow, my child, in body chosen
Of the God who made the earth;
Mine the answer, in confusion,
Young, unready to give birth;

Lullaby, lullaby,
God awaits a baby's cry,
Lullaby.

Sleep, my child, this friendly manger
Guards your weak and tender age;
Childhood brings such fearful danger,
War, disease, and famine rage;
Lullaby, lullaby,
Word of God in baby's cry,
Lullaby.

Slumber still, for love surrounds us,
We have not been left alone.
Though disgrace and shame may hound us,
Joseph stays and shields his own;
Lullaby, lullaby,
Word of God in baby's cry,
Lullaby.

Hush, my child, God's grace protect you
From coercion, hate and power;
As you grow, let love direct you,
Shape your living, hour by hour;
Lullaby, lullaby,
Hope of God in mother's cry,
Lullaby.

Wake, my child, the world is crying,
Calls you, evil's power to cross,
Opens you to early dying,
Motherhood's most dreaded loss;
    Lullaby, lullaby,
    Hope of God in mother's cry,
    Lullaby.

DANIEL

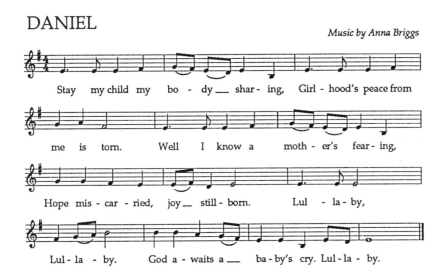

Music by Anna Briggs

Stay my child my bo - dy __ shar - ing, Girl - hood's peace from me is torn. Well I know a moth - er's fear - ing, Hope mis - car - ried, joy __ still - born. Lul - la - by, Lul - la - by. God a - waits a __ ba - by's cry. Lul - la - by.

*Anna Briggs
is a writer and artist
and member of the
Iona Community,
who lives in
Springhill, N.S.*

Beth Percival,
Julie Dodd,
Margaret Ashford,
Jill Lightwood,
Lyle Brehaut,
Charlottetown,
P.E.I.

I Am Pieces

Beth Sewell

I am daughter, child, learner,
Unknowing, clumsy, inept,
I am the one who can't.

I am teacher, healer, mother,
Remembering, guiding, carrying,
I am the one who answers.

I am volunteer, driver, sorter,
Caring, doing, working,
I am the one who says yes.

I am listener, helper, friend,
Sharing, loving, hearing,
I am the one who cares.

I am fragmented, pulled, twisted,
Turning, whirling, spinning,
I am the one in pieces.

Beth Sewell is the
pseudonym
of an Ontario
churchwoman.

Linda Ervin, United Church minister, Vancouver.

Letter to My Friends

Clare Christie

Singleness is a justice issue. And as an "always single" woman, I am part of the group that is valued the least among (white) women in our society.

The fact that I don't buy in to this devalued image is a tribute to my upbringing, my family and friends, and myself. But those same family and friends, that same self, have never affirmed and celebrated my singleness.

To be a complete person is not dependent upon a lasting marriage relationship (notice that I didn't write "happy") but rather upon a well-developed sense of self-esteem, a personal strength of integrity, without smugness or intolerance. Wholeness is integration of mind, body, and spirit.

As a single person, I have the opportunity to find solitude, and in solitude, to know myself psychologically, intellectually, and spiritually, as well as physically. Solitude offers the opportunity to pass through pain to growth.

As a single person I have to take responsibility for my decisions and actions and am forced into honesty.

One of the reasons I celebrate my singleness is that I cherish the opportunity to be myself. I affirm that I desire always to be "single," even as I long to share with other "singles" of both sexes and sexual orientations, all religions and races, all ages and physical and mental capacities, and of whatever marital status.

In sharing on an intimate level, I meet my God, the goodness in all people, and I feel blessed.

Sexual intimacy, especially in marriage, would be the ultimate sharing, but to find a "single," a whole person who is also male, unmarried, heterosexual, and local, feels at times a little like believing that fairy tales come true. *Sometimes* they do, but in the meantime, as an uncoupled single, I can make my own decisions about developing and balancing my glorious opportunities: for solitude or to enjoy a wealth of intimacy with my family and friends and in my professional life.

It is time for society, and all the individuals society comprises, including singles ourselves, to recognize individual worth, to accept people as individuals, and to plan public and social functions so that all individuals feel welcomed and accepted. It should be acceptable for people to go to public events by themselves, to attend social functions without an escort, to remain single, to divorce, and to be widowed.

Couples who don't develop single friends miss a great resource! Whether we are heterosexual or homosexual, what difference should that make?

Single people would be well advised to live life to the fullest with what they have at hand — themselves — rather than operating with a "camping mentality," ready to pull up stakes when a potential mate materializes. Years can pass with many opportunities missed.

Fecundity is not only a matter of bearing and raising children. Loving others and receiving their love, allowing them the gift of giving, is a fecundity denied to no one. In my singleness, I affirm my capacity to love and to be loved. Next time I am asked, "How's your love life?", I'll respond that it is abundant and rich in its variety!

Singlehood is a justice issue. Accept and respect us.

Clare Christie, who lives in Halifax, is a lawyer, a feminist, and a single woman to whom the spiritual dimension of life is the most important.

Grandma

Lynda Katsuno-Ishii

Grandma, my first conscious memories of you are of running up the street to greet you after work when I was a child, always hoping that you had some little gift for me. I realize now the most precious of all the gifts you gave were in the hug and the love you gave me each day and all through my life.

Love is a prayer, Grandma, and I offer this to you with the deepest love and respect.

All the earth is a womb, and in this space of life, you became like a tree. You came to this country as a young bride from Japan and planted seeds that gave roots to work, a family, a life. It was not at all an easy life. Yet you sent your roots of love and faith deep down into the earth, where they grew and became strong, sustaining and supporting us through the sunshine and the rain, the darkness and the light of each of our lives. You were always there for us, and I will always hold you up as someone so Christ-like in nature. Christ incarnate was always found in you.

You also sent your branches up into the sky, reaching up, spreading out, growing, strengthening, and bearing the fruits that have been passed on to each generation. These fruits, these gifts, have sheltered us and nourished us and touched the lives of others in this forest of life.

When a branch was broken, you groaned and wept, and the sap from your body flowed like tears, but your roots of love always helped to restore, strengthen, and heal. This became clear during the very difficult time following my car accident (which left me to depend on four wheels to zoom around this world). You said once, near the end of your life, that you had received so much "courage" from me, and I remember replying that it was only "recycled courage"!

I remember numerous times of leaving you. Now, at your departing from the space of time that we call life, I weep tears of love and deep thanks for all you were and all you gave to us. You, the tree of life, have left us, but we will use our tears to water and nourish the seeds and the roots that you have left behind.

In memory of grandparents Teruko Ishii and Chiaki Katsuno, first generation Japanese-Canadians.

Lynda Katsuno-Ishii is a teacher and musician who recently returned to Canada after working for seven years with the World Council of Churches in Geneva.

Hands of
Elizabeth Welch,
Port Kirwin, Nfld.

A Prayer for Mother's Day

Catherine Stewart-Kroeker

Gracious and loving God, we thank you for the love that we have known through all who have been mothers. Sometimes it has been meagre and measured, sometimes overwhelming like a mighty river. Sometimes it has come as discipline or anger, sometimes as gentle compassion and sensitivity, a kind touch, a cradling care. For that love which we have known, we give thanks.

We thank you for the love of foster parents, whose task is often brief and thankless. We thank you for adoptive parents, who choose to share their lives with a child birthed by another. For their love, O God, we give you thanks.

We thank you for pregnancy, for the privilege of being able to experience so intimately the miracle of new life, for the joy of hearing the heart beat for the first time, the excitement of the first kicks of a life that is within. Yet we cannot forget those who experience pregnancy as a physical and emotional disaster: who feel continually nauseated, who feel frustrated with their awkwardness and fatigue, who have reason to worry about the health of their baby. For all women who are with child, we pray your blessings, O God.

We also know of many women who long to bear children, yet for unknown reasons it seems physically impossible. For them, we pray for a sense of peace.

We pray for those women who have known the death of a child within their womb, before it could be fully formed. Grant to them a community that will mourn with them and recognize the reality of that life only the mother has known.

We pray for those who have become mothers through unhappy circumstances and for our society that gives very mixed signals to women about who they are and why they are valuable, and so contributes to this malaise surrounding our sexuality. Grant us all great wisdom, compassion, and insight, as we try to perceive and mediate your word in this confusion.

We pray for parents who have seen their expectations for their children shattered and are struggling to know that each child is a gift, whose life they do not control. We think of those who have lost children through accident or illness; and of those who feel they have lost a child because the child has chosen a life so different from their own. We pray for an outpouring of your truth and love.

We pray for parents who are being blamed for their children's faults, and who review the past endlessly, wondering where things went wrong. We pray that they might acknowledge their failures and area of responsibility, yet also be able to see the boundaries between their responsibilities and those of their child.

We pray for mothers who have put all their life energy into rearing their children and now face a massive reorientation as their children leave home. Grant them courage, we pray.

We pray for mothers around the world whose worries seem much more basic than our own: for mothers in war zones who worry simply about their children's daily survival; for mothers who bring children into the world knowing that it is only a matter of time until they die of malnutrition.

O God, were we able to hear all the cries that arise from the hearts and lips of mothers around the world, we would not be able to bear the pain. Can it be that you can bear all this pain? Your love, O God, has been described as like the love of a mother: as the womb protects and nurtures, but does not possess and control, so is your love for us, O God. You have formed us in the womb, borne us, and carried us from the womb even to our old age. You promise: "I have made, and I will bear. I will carry and I will save."

And so we praise you, O good and loving God; we put our trust in you; in you do we place our hope. All praise, glory, and honour be to you, most gracious and compassionate God, our help and our redeemer. Amen.

Catherine
Stewart-Kroeker
is a minister of
St. Cuthbert's
Presbyterian
Church, Hamilton,
Ont., and the
mother of three.

Telling stories,
Spence Bay, N.W.T.

Conspiracy*

Margo Ritchie, c.s.j.

Come, join the conspiracy ...
Together, let's conspire!
Shallow breath,
Caught by twentieth century air.
The air of twenty centuries, trapped in our lungs.
Tightened chest,
Labouring lungs,
Straining to enlargen.
Narrow constrictions gripping us,
The narrow passageways of half-thought thoughts,
Of half-dreamed dreams, of half-loved loves,
Of half-schemed schemes.
Let go the fortress-held stance of shallowly-breathed patterns.
Breathe deeply now.
Echoes of another call ...
Come and see!
Now ... come and breathe.
Yes! Come join the conspiracy ...
Together, let us conspire!

Margo Ritchie is a woman committed to the struggle to create a better world, who works at Medaille House spirituality centre in London, Ont.

*The Latin root of the word conspiracy means to breathe together.

In Love Revealed

Anna Briggs

Suggested tunes: "Surrey" or "Melita"

The busy crowd was thronging 'round.
A frightened woman, cursed for years,
Pushed through the throng and, trembling still,
Reached out and found you through her tears;
She touched your hem, and she was healed.
Behold, God's grace in love revealed.

The little girl was fading fast.
Her father dragged you to his door.
You banished those who wept and wailed;
She rose up, live and whole once more.
You kissed her cheek, and she was healed.
Behold, God's grace in love revealed.

They brought her to you to be stoned,
The woman caught in act of shame;
You turned their judgment into care
And gave forgiveness, took her blame;
You touched her heart, and she was healed.
Behold, God's grace in love revealed.

The woman at the well was kind,
Though doubly outcast, did not shrink.
You told her of the spirit's need
For love more strong than food or drink;
You drank her cup, and she was healed;
Behold, God's grace in love revealed.

The women, weeping, found the tomb,
Your body gone, the stone laid by;
You bade them tell the brothers how
Your love in death could never die;
They told the news, and all were healed.
Behold, God's grace in love revealed.

Through centuries of scorn and shame
Your love has named us as your own;
Through poverty, despair, and fear
Our faith and hopefulness have grown;
You touch us all, and we are healed,
Behold, God's grace in love revealed.

*Anna Briggs
is a writer and
artist and a member
of the Iona
Community,
who lives in
Springhill, N.S.*

Knitting mill,
Toronto.

To Maria Jose, Where Are You?

Nela Rio
(translated by J. Weiss and A. Mason)

I ask myself
you ask yourself
we still ask ourselves
if this life that keeps moving on
includes me
includes you
precludes us.

In the long hours descending slowly into routine
when the questions become threaded in the life of every day
I pretend
we pretend to live as if this normality were
a gift.

They do not understand
— will they understand? —
that if normality does not include you
does not include us all
it is madness
and the world must run to the edge of itself and commit suicide.

How to live the days
how to sleep the nights

how to find answers organize plan celebrate changes
if you are not here if all of us are not here any longer.

How to hold
the words
with kindness tenderness beauty honour and respect
the memories
of so many lives given giving to the world in order to create life in the
lives that live without living.

How can the revolution be a victory if the world we make together
does not include me
does not include you
precludes us?
How can we believe the victory is a revolution
— nothing changes never will —
if the new eternal always woman woman
has to keep on fighting in the revolution just won.

It is the lives of these deaths
that give life.

I say to you
woman
I do remember us.

*Nela Rio is an
Argentina-born
professor of Spanish-
American literature
at St. Thomas
University,
Fredericton, N.B.*

Child of God

Dorothy MacNeill

Suggested tune: "Sons of God"

Child of God, choices must be made,
We must work as hard as we have prayed.
Find the courage, realize
Life is great, life is our prize,
Allelu, allelu, allelu, allelu, alleluia.

Sister, neighbour, let's be one
Sharing things that must be done.
Work from rise to set of sun,
Separately, together.

Child of God, choices must be made,
We must work as hard as we have prayed.
Find the courage, realize
Life is great, life is our prize,
Allelu, allelu, allelu, allelu, alleluia.

Shout and sing with loudest praise,
To our God our voices raise.
Life may seem a puzzling maze,
But we're here together.

Child of God, choices must be made,
We must work as hard as we have prayed.
Find the courage, realize
Life is great, life is our prize,
Allelu, allelu, allelu, allelu, alleluia.

God, Creator of all things,
Jesus, our redemption brings,
In our lives the Spirit sings,
As we stand together.

Child of God, choices must be made,
We must work as hard as we have prayed.
Find the courage, realize
Life is great, life is our prize,
Allelu, allelu, allelu, allelu, alleluia.

*Dorothy MacNeill
is a "former
everything," who
now works part time
at the Atlantic
School of Theology,
Halifax, while
continuing her work
as a volunteer.*

Marcia Braundy,
carpenter and
activist,
Vallican, B.C.

Let Us Now Praise Courageous Women

Edith Shore

When I think about the women who are part of my life, I am overcome by their gifts, their energy, their intelligence, their determination, their joy, and their grief. They are like a litany of saints or a rosary of friends who strengthen me as I repeat their names and name their circumstances.

When we pray, thinking of these women, we begin with a prayer rooted in our own needs. Finding the face of God in them, we strengthen the divine in our own lives.

We pray for ourselves:

That we may have the strength of Diane, who is dyslexic and mildly retarded but manages home and family, work, and aging parents, and still smiles.

Creator of all, renew us.

That we may have the energy and determination of Madeleine, who pursues a career based on her own wonderful musical talent, although promoting herself and being close to many people depletes her energy.

Creator of all, renew us.

That we may have the quiet dignity and openness of Margaret, who is a deeply committed Christian and is married to a man of a different faith and a different and currently unpopular nationality.

Creator of all, renew us.

That we may have the tested character of Gwen, who left her vocation to the ministry and faced alienation in order to maintain the lesbian partnership in which she found affirmation and love.

Creator of all, renew us.

That we may have the quiet and cheerful staying power of Anna, who is divorced and doing a full-time job after years of volunteer work and whose gifts of music and personal generosity are a light to her co-workers.

Creator of all, renew us.

That we may have the courage and joy of Dorothy, who, from her wheelchair, works for peace all over the world and brings a role model to differently abled people, as well as new insight to those of us who consider ourselves whole.

Creator of all, renew us.

We pray for the friends who light our way along the complicated and treacherous passages that many of us must take. We do well to stand in awe of the raw courage and fortitude of these women. We pray that God will nourish, bless, anoint, refresh, and strengthen each of them:

Mary, who lives on her deathbed, unexpectedly struck down by a massive cancer in the midst of raising her family and working at a demanding job that is focussed on helping others.

Redeemer of all, give your strength and the power of your healing love.

Eleanor, who is in the midst of a painful and protracted transition from childhood to adulthood, moving out of a long and unhappy marriage into a frightening future, seeking and discovering her real strengths at long last.

Redeemer of all, give your strength and the power of your healing love.

Ruth, whose husband of twenty-seven years died very suddenly of AIDS, without anyone knowing about his bisexuality and without more than a few minutes in which the two could talk together.

Redeemer of all, give your strength and the power of your healing love.

Catherine, whose beautiful young daughter was cut down by the bullets of a deranged boyfriend, and who courageously faces a future that will always include that loss.

Redeemer of all, give your strength and the power of your healing love.

Florence, a young Native woman, whose great gifts of oratory, passion, and determination will be needed as she faces a life of struggle against racism, deceit, and the devastation of her people.

Redeemer of all, give your strength and the power of your healing love.

The unnamed woman among us, who makes her living by prostitution and deals daily with the unwillingness of our society to be more whole about sexuality and more loving in our moral deliberations.

Redeemer of all, give your strength and the power of your healing love.

We give thanks for the women who are young, beautiful, and full of the celebration of life ahead; for the women who are old and beautiful and full of the wisdom of life lived; for the women who are no longer with us in this life but who were our grandmothers, our mothers, our mentors, and those who pioneered many of our freedoms:

For Jennifer, who is retired and arthritic but works tirelessly at the unfairness and inhumanity of the law and who does volunteer work that reflects her commitment and her extensive background.

Life-giving Spirit, we give you thanks.

For Wendy, who, like other young and inexperienced women, is finding a way through life with different sexual norms and different career demands than those of her mother and grandmother.

Life-giving Spirit, we give you thanks.

For Lorraine, who not only survived a late-life divorce but made it the beginning of a new educational adventure for herself and of new achievements in helping church members through the wilderness of divorce.

Life-giving Spirit, we give you thanks.

For Sophie, who is intelligent, young, well-trained in several athletic disciplines, and who has gifts of good and easy relationships, quick enthusiasm for life, and cheerful confidence in the future.

Life-giving Spirit, we give you thanks.

For my mother, who overcame a childhood home lacking in warmth and a mediocre education, who gave to her own children the affection that was denied to her, and continued her own education until the end of her life.

Life-giving Spirit, we give you thanks.

For our daughters, whose lives and potential give us great hope for the future, and whose struggles to be whole in a world that is complex, patriarchal, and destructive initiate us into the pain of creation and the joy of being part of their journeys.

Life-giving Spirit, we give you thanks.

Amen.

*Edith Shore
is a consultant for
the Anglican Church
of Canada on human
rights, justice
and corrections,
and AIDS.*

Mary O'Brien,
philosopher and
theorist, speaking at
Toronto.

La Colombe Prend Son Vol

Gordon Light
(translated by Robert Faerber)

Sur ses ailes déployées
auréolées de soleil
elle prend son envolée
dans le vent.
Et au sein de l'obscurité
son chant fait vibrer la nuit
plein de rire et de lumière
dans le vent.

Et les eaux se bercent
à l'aube du premier jour
comme un berceau vide paré pour la vie
pour la vie.
Et du coeur de Dieu l'Esprit se répand sur la terre entière
une mère soufflant vie dans son enfant.

Nombreux sont les rêveurs
qui ont retrouvé leur vie
quand l'Esprit aux rêves donna forme et vie,
forme et vie.
Les déserts sont refleuris, les coeurs brisés retrouvent joie.
La colombe reprend son vol dans le temps.

Et la douce brise
caressa la jeune fille,
un murmure dans la nuit de son destin,
son destin,
Une promesse de paix dans un enfant au règne sans fin
Et le coeur de Marie déborda de chant.

La blanche colombe
vers le Jourdain prit son vol
et plana sur le jeune homme plein de grâce,
plein de grâce,
et descendit sur lui qui sortait de l'eau de son baptème
et l'entoura de son souffle tout puissant.

Vint la nuit obscure
qui enveloppa la terre
et puis l'aube en feu du soleil du matin,
du matin,
à nouveau l'Esprit toucha la terre ailes déployées
apportant vie par le feu et par le vent.

SHE FLIES ON!

Words & Music by
Gordon Light

She comes sail-ing on the wind, Her wings flash-ing in the sun, On a jour-ney just be-gun, She flies on.____ And in the pass-age of her flight, her song rings out through the night, full of laugh-ter,____ full of light, She flies on!_____

(3rd & 5th verses)

1. Sil-ent wat-ers rock-ing ____ on the morn-ing of our birth, Like an emp-ty cra-dle wait-ing to be filled, (to be filled). And from the heart of God, the Spi-rit moved up-on the earth, Like a mo-ther breath-ing life in-to her child. She comes

D.S.

2. Many were the dreamers whose eyes were given sight,
When the Spirit filled their dreams with life and form, (life and form).
Deserts turned to gardens, broken hearts found new delight,
And then down the ages, still, She flew on.

3. To a gentle girl from Galilee, a gentle breeze she came,
A whisper softly calling in the dark, (in the dark).
The promise of a child of Peace, whose reign would never end,
Mary sang the Spirit song within her heart.

4. Flying to the river, she waited circling high,
Above the child now grown so full of grace, (full of grace).
As he rose up from the water, she swept down from the sky,
And she carried him away in her embrace.

5. Long after the deep darkness that fell upon the world,
After dawn returned in flame of rising sun, (rising sun).
The Spirit touched the earth again, again her wings unfurled,
Bringing life in wind and fire as she flew on.

Gordon Light
is a dean of the
Anglican Church
in Kamloops, B.C.

Joella Foulds,
musician,
broadcaster,
activist,
Sydney, N.S.

Printed in Canada

920059